This Is Our FAMILY

Memories to Cherish for a Lifetime

RUBY OAKS

Castle Point Books
New York

www.stmartins.com
www.castlepointbooks.com

The Castle Point Books trademark is owned by Castle Point Publications, LLC.
Castle Point books are published and distributed by St. Martin's Press.

ISBN 978-1-250-21510-9 (hardcover)

Cover design by Katie Jennings Campbell
Interior design by Joanna Williams

Images used under license from Shutterstock.com

Our books may be purchased in bulk for promotional, educational, or business use.
Please contact your local bookseller or the Macmillan Corporate and Premium Sales
Department at
1-800-221-7945, extension 5442, or by email at MacmillanSpecialMarkets@macmillan.com.

First Edition: May 2019

10 9 8 7 6 5 4 3 2 1

CONTENTS

INTRODUCTION

Every family has a story...

Well, maybe *lots* of stories. Some may make you smile or laugh. Others may bring tears to your eyes. Many are simply the stories of everyday life—in the car, around the dinner table, in the backyard—that make up most of our time together. All of these have immeasurable value because they are moments you have shared with the people you love most in the world.

There is no right or wrong way to keep a record of your family's stories: big and small, happy and heartfelt, past and present. What is important is what you are doing right now: writing down as much as you can remember so you can revisit each wonderful moment whenever you like.

We always believe that special family memories will stay in our hearts and minds. This book will help ensure that is true for you. If you are filling it out in retrospect, the prompts on these pages will bring back a rush of emotions and mental pictures. If you are jotting down notes as the events happen, you will find yourself appreciating each moment more as you realize just how many little things truly do mean a lot. Hold to the task and see it through, and the blank book in your hands will transform into a cherished family heirloom—a very special keepsake of a story that is beautifully, uniquely your own.

Family
is not an
important thing.
It's everything.

—MICHAEL J. FOX

OUR
FAMILY
& FRIENDS
TREE

This Is Our Family

Once Upon a Time...

LOOK AT US WHEN WE WERE JUST A FAMILY OF TWO.

Date we met:

_____

Where we met:

_____

Date we married:

_____

...Then Our Family Grew!

HERE IS A PHOTO OF OUR WHOLE FAMILY.

Who is in the photo:

Where it was taken:

What was happening at the time:

The Stars of This Story

Full name:

Nicknames:

Birthday:

Full name:

Nicknames:

Birthday:

Full name:

Nicknames:

Birthday:

Full name:

Nicknames:

Birthday:

Full name:

Nicknames:

Birthday:

Full name:

Nicknames:

Birthday:

7

Our Family Heritage

We can trace our story back through generations.

COUNTRIES OUR ANCESTORS CAME FROM:

_____

_____

_____

WHAT WE KNOW ABOUT OUR FAMILY NAME(S):

_____

_____

_____

WAYS WE CELEBRATE OUR SHARED HERITAGE:

_____

_____

_____

a family secret

Here's a story about one of our ancestors:

Heirlooms & Keepsakes

Discover these treasures that have been passed
down through the years.

[Item:

[Belonged to:

[Item:

[Belonged to:

[Item:

[Belonged to:

[Item:

[Belonged to:

[Item:

[Belonged to:

Our Family Connections

Meet some of our closest family members.

family fun
Look through some
old photos with the whole
family to see how many
of these people
you can find!

Our Family Zoo

We've had a few fur babies, finned friends,
and other animals who won our hearts.

PET NAME: _____

Breed: _____

Nicknames: _____

Best (& worst) traits: _____

_____

_____

PET NAME: _____

Breed: _____

Nicknames: _____

Best (& worst) traits: _____

_____

_____

The Best of Friends

We have many special people in our lives
who feel as close as family.

CHILDHOOD BUDDIES:

special neighbors:

FRIENDS WHO ARE LIKE FAMILY:

Caring & Sharing

These caregivers, mentors, and teachers
went the extra mile for our family.

BEST BABYSITTERS:

_____

_____

_____

MEANINGFUL MENTORS:

_____

_____

_____

TOP TEACHERS:

_____

_____

_____

KIND CAREGIVERS:

_____

_____

_____

Special Guests

We welcomed some people dear to us to stay
in our home and spend time with our family.

Our Guest(s)	Date(s) of Visit	Occasion/ Reason	A Memory

Celebrity Sightings

These famous folks crossed paths with
our family at one time or another.

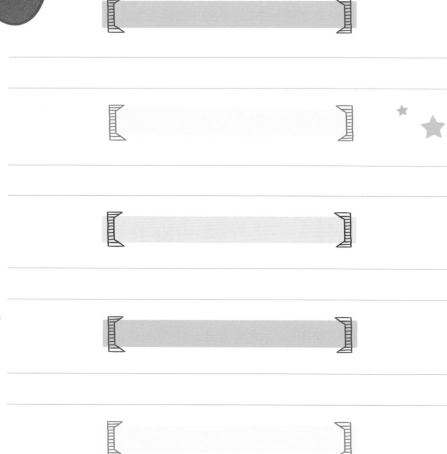

According to Us

What do we each think about our family?

THE THREE WORDS THAT BEST DESCRIBE OUR FAMILY:

1. _____
2. _____
3. _____
Says: _____

1. _____
2. _____
3. _____
Says: _____

1. _____
2. _____
3. _____
Says: _____

1. _____
2. _____
3. _____
Says: _____

IF WE HAD A FAMILY MOTTO, IT WOULD BE:

_____
_____
_____
Says: _____
_____
_____
Says: _____

_____
_____
_____
Says: _____
_____
_____
Says: _____

I have a
wonderful shelter,
which is
my family.

—JOSE CARRERAS

PLACES
IN OUR
HEARTS

Homemade Memories

This is the home where our family
spent the most years.

OUR ADDRESS:

_____

YEARS WE LIVED THERE:

_____

A FAVORITE MEMORY (OR TWO) OF THIS HOME:

_____

_____

Stops Along the Way

Over the years, we also have had these roofs over our heads—before or after we all came together.

Address: _____

Type of home: _____

When we lived there: _____

A favorite memory: _____

Address: _____

Type of home: _____

When we lived there: _____

A favorite memory: _____

Address: _____

Type of home: _____

When we lived there: _____

A favorite memory: _____

Address: _____

Type of home: _____

When we lived there: _____

A favorite memory: _____

Our Gathering Spaces

Our rooms are filled with so many memories.

IN THE KITCHEN

_____

_____

IN THE DINING ROOM

_____

_____

IN THE LIVING ROOM

_____

_____

IN THE FAMILY ROOM

_____

_____

IN ANOTHER FAVORITE ROOM: _____

_____

_____

Always Welcome

Here are the homes of family and friends
where we can drop in or even stay.

[_____ 'S HOUSE]

Where it is:

Why we go there:

A memory:

[_____ 'S HOUSE]

Where it is:

Why we go there:

A memory:

[_____ 'S HOUSE]

Where it is:

Why we go there:

A memory:

[_____ 'S HOUSE]

Where it is:

Why we go there:

A memory:

Favorite Hangouts

These sites bring to mind special
family memories and stories.

AN OUTDOOR SPACE:

_____

It's special because: _____

INDOOR ENTERTAINMENT:

_____

It's special because: _____

a place to eat:

It's special because:

BIT OF CULTURE:

_____

It's special because: _____

ANOTHER FAVORITE HAUNT:

_____

It's special because: _____

All Around Town

From A to Z, here are a few places our family
goes to get out of the house!

Afternoon outing: _____

Bike riding: _____

Bookstore: _____

Dessert spot: _____

Grocery store: _____

Hiking: _____

Kids' food: _____

Kids' haircut: _____

Library: _____

Other local spots we love:

Mall: _____

Mini golf: _____

Movie theater: _____

Museum: _____

Park: _____

Pizza place: _____

Playground: _____

Zoo or farm: _____

_____

_____

_____

Our Travel Adventures

In our journey as a family,
we have visited these places.

DESTINATION:

_____

When we went:_____

How we got there:_____

Where we stayed:_____

Three things we did:
1._____   2._____   3._____

One thing we'd do if we went back:

_____

DESTINATION:

_____

When we went:_____

How we got there:_____

Where we stayed:_____

Three things we did:
1._____   2._____   3._____

One thing we'd do if we went back:

_____

DESTINATION:

_____

When we went: _____

How we got there: _____

Where we stayed: _____

Three things we did:

1. _____ 2. _____ 3. _____

One thing we'd do if we went back:

_____

a family secret

We can never leave home without:

Day Trips
& Weekend Getaways

Little trips also brought our family big fun.
Here is a favorite place we visited.

DESTINATION:

_____

WHEN WE WENT: HOW WE GOT THERE:

_____

A FAVORITE ACTIVITY OR MEMORY:

_____

School Days

Beyond academics, these places helped our family
discover friendships, talents, and interests.

OUR PRESCHOOL(S):

_____

OUR ELEMENTARY SCHOOL(S):

_____

OUR MIDDLE SCHOOL(S):

_____

OUR HIGH SCHOOL(S):

_____

OTHER LEARNING CENTERS:

_____

_____

_____

_____

_____

On Campus

Club meetings and events, sports and rec, arts and performances—here are the spots at school where our family felt most at home.

ASSEMBLIES IN THE AUDITORIUM:

_____

_____

events in the gym:

MEMORIES FROM THE STADIUM:

_____

_____

FAVORITE SCHOOL EVENTS:

_____

_____

OTHER SPECIAL PLACES ON CAMPUS:

 _____

_____

Activity Centers

We put a lot of miles on, going to and from
sports, hobbies, classes, and meetings!

ACADEMICS & TUTORING:

_____

_____

_____

_____

SPORTS & FITNESS:

_____

_____

_____

_____

VISUAL & PERFORMING ARTS:

_____

_____

_____

_____

The family
is link to
our past, bridge
to our future.

—ALEX HALEY

SPECIAL DAYS, TRADITIONS & CELEBRATIONS

Birthday Traditions

Our family celebrates birthdays in our own special way!

FAVORITE CELEBRATION LOCATIONS:

_____

_____

FUN PARTY THEMES:

_____

_____

MUST-HAVE BIRTHDAY FOODS:

_____

_____

BEST BIRTHDAY GAMES AND ACTIVITIES:

_____

_____

family fun

Some of the best birthday presents our family
has shared with each other:

Our Birthday "Firsts"

Here are photos from first birthdays.
Yes—parents, too!

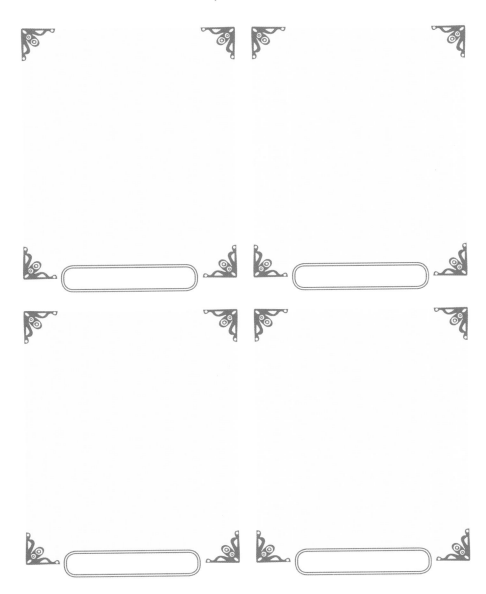

Ringing in the New Year

Celebrating the New Year as a family can be special—
no matter if everyone makes it to midnight.

A MEMORABLE NEW YEAR'S EVE AS A FAMILY:

where we were:

HOW WE CELEBRATED:

HOW LATE WE STAYED UP:

Springtime Celebrations

These are a few of our favorite ways
to welcome the season.

- Planting a garden
- Jumping in puddles
- Playing in the rain or mud
- Visiting playgrounds
- Seeing the cherry blossoms
- Going for a bike ride

- Flying kites
- Picking flowers
- Blowing bubbles
- Drawing with sidewalk chalk
- Feeding ducks
- Chasing rainbows

OTHER WARM-WEATHER FUN:

_____

_____

_____

family fun

Our favorite springtime holiday is:

How we celebrate:

Mother's Day Memories

It's easy to make Mom feel special. Here are a few things that work best—*besides* hugs, kisses, and cards.

A MOTHER'S DAY PHOTO:

HANDMADE GIFTS AND GOODIES:

_____

_____

A FAVORITE MEMORY FROM MOM:

_____

_____

Father's Day Memories

Dad loves to be loved, too. Here are some ways the family shows how they really feel.

A FATHER'S DAY PHOTO:

HANDMADE GIFTS AND GOODIES:

_____

_____

A FAVORITE MEMORY FROM DAD:

_____

_____

Family on the Fourth

This is our family's idea of having a blast
on the birthday of America.

A FOURTH OF JULY PHOTO:

PICNICS & EVENTS WE'VE ATTENDED:

_____

_____

a family secret

Our favorite spot for fireworks:

Summer Fun

School's out! Here are a few ways we make
the most of the break—and the weather.

- Playing in a sprinkler or pool
- Working in the garden
- Eating watermelon
- Going to festivals and fairs
- Taking a nature walk
- Sleeping under the stars
- Having a lemonade stand
- Going to drive-in movies
- Attending a sports event

- Playing outdoor sports or games
- Attending an outdoor concert
- Having a yard sale
- Going fishing
- Enjoying ice cream
- Picking berries at a farm
- Visiting amusement parks
- Gathering around a campfire

OTHER SUMMERTIME FUN:

Halloween Treats

How much fun we've had each holiday!

OUR TYPICAL HALLOWEEN:

_____

_____

_____

_____

_____

FAVORITE COSTUMES OVER THE YEARS:

_____

_____

_____

_____

_____

a family secret

Parents' favorite treats to steal:

42

Autumn Adventures

These are the reasons our family loves fall.

- Picking apples
- Carving jack-o'-lanterns
- Painting pumpkins
- Attending fall sports
- Sipping cider
- Going on a hayride
- Jumping in a leaf pile
- Buying new school supplies
- Going to a harvest fest
- Winding through a corn maze

- Signing up for a charity race
- Making chili or soup
- Visiting a spooky spot
- Watching Halloween shows
- Having a campfire

family fun

Best fall festival:

Best spooky fun:

OTHER FALL-WEATHER FUN:

Thanksgiving Get-Togethers

We are grateful for these memories of
our time around the harvest table.

Thanksgiving dinners
are usually held here:

THIS IS WHAT IS USUALLY SERVED:

_____

_____

THIS IS WHAT THE KIDS ACTUALLY EAT:

_____

_____

a family secret
One of our family's favorite recipes:

Winter Happenings

The days may grow shorter, but we
still enjoy lots of wintertime fun.

- Playing in the snow
- Going ice-skating
- Making paper snowflakes
- Baking cookies
- Enjoying outdoor sports

- Cuddling around a fireplace
- Helping people in need
- Decorating
- Making homemade gifts
- Singing (or hearing) carols

✳ OTHER WINTRY DOINGS:

_____

_____

_____

family fun

A place we love to go to celebrate the holiday season:

Happy Holidays

Here is our favorite wintertime holiday
and how we celebrate.

OUR FAMILY PHOTO FROM THIS HOLIDAY:

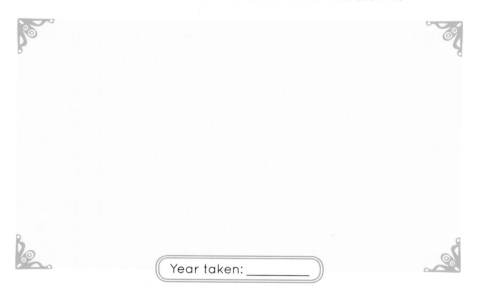

Year taken: _____

OUR HOLIDAY ALWAYS INCLUDES:

_____

_____

family fun

The best gift we ever received as a family:

The Gang's All Here

From great-aunts to cousin-friends, our extended
family holds special meaning and memories.
These are a few times we have gotten together.

WEDDINGS & ANNIVERSARIES:

_____

_____

FAMILY REUNIONS:

_____

_____

BIG FAMILY TRIPS:

_____

_____

_____

_____

Saying Goodbye

Here are some people who filled our lives with love
and laughter while they were with us.

Full name:

Born: Died:

Favorite trait:

Full name:

Born: Died:

Favorite trait:

Full name:

Born: Died:

Favorite trait:

Full name:

Born: Died:

Favorite trait:

SOME OF THE WAYS WE CELEBRATE AND
PAY TRIBUTE AT A MEMORIAL SERVICE:

FAMILY FUN
& GAMES

Backyard Activities

Some of our fondest memories are of time
spent right in our own backyard.

HERE IS OUR FAMILY PLAYING OUTSIDE:

WE PLAYED THESE SPORTS:

_____

_____

_____

_____

_____

WE ENJOYED THESE OUTDOOR ACTIVITIES:

_____

_____

_____

_____

THE KIDS WERE ONLY ALLOWED TO DO
THESE MESSY THINGS OUTSIDE:

_____

_____

_____

_____

In the Playroom

We won't always have plastic building blocks under foot. Here's what we want to remember about what it was like.

HERE ARE THE KIDS HARD AT PLAY
(OR MESS!) WITH THEIR TOYS:

THESE ARE A FEW FAVORITE TOYS
THAT AREN'T SHOWN:

_____

_____

WE ALSO LOVE THESE PRETEND GAMES:

_____

_____

The Family Talent Show

Kid performances may be planned or impromptu, but they always make us smile.

THESE ARE SOME WAYS OUR KIDS LIKE TO ENTERTAIN US:

- Singing and dancing
- Putting on a play they wrote
- Acting out a TV show or movie

- Doing magic tricks
- Doing sports or stunts
- Telling jokes

OTHER TYPES OF SHOWS HAVE INCLUDED:

Movie Memories

Screen time can be family time
when we watch together.

MOVIES WE SAW AT THE THEATER:

_____

_____

WE ENJOYED THESE MOVIE-NIGHT TRADITIONS
(WHETHER AT HOME OR IN THE THEATER):

_____

_____

WE CONSIDER THESE MOVIES CLASSICS:

_____

_____

a family secret

Movie lines we quote to each other:

TV Together

Our top-rated shows have changed over the years, but these are our all-time favorites.

FAVORITE TODDLER SHOWS:

favorite kids' shows:

FAVORITE TWEEN AND TEEN SHOWS:

SPORTS PLAYOFFS AND AWARDS
SHOWS WE NEVER MISSED:

On the Bookshelf

These are the books that were
dog-eared from many a reading.

FAVORITE BOARD BOOKS:

_____

_____

_____

favorite preschooler books:

FAVORITE LEARNING-TO-READ BOOKS:

_____

_____

_____

FAVORITE CHAPTER BOOKS:

_____

_____

_____

HERE ARE SOME OF THE BEST QUOTES
FROM THESE KIDS' BOOKS:

" _____ "

" _____ "

" _____ "

" _____ "

THESE ARE THE CHARACTERS FROM BOOKS
THAT REMIND US OF EACH FAMILY MEMBER:

Mom acts like _____ in the book _____
written by _____

Dad acts like _____ in the book _____
by _____

_____ acts like _____ in _____
by _____

_____ acts like _____ in _____
by _____

_____ acts like _____ in _____
by _____

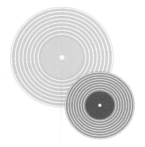

Our Family Soundtrack

Here is the music that brings back
memories for our family.

THESE SONGS AND ARTISTS GOT PLENTY OF PLAY TIME AT HOME:

_____

_____

_____

_____

_____

_____

_____

AS A FAMILY, WE WENT TO SEE THESE SINGERS AND BANDS PERFORM:

_____

_____

_____

_____

THESE ARE A FEW SONGS WE TAUGHT THE KIDS:

_____

_____

_____

_____

OUR FAVORITE (REAL OR PRETEND)
INSTRUMENTS TO PLAY:

_____

_____

_____

_____

family fun
If we wanted a dance party to break out,
this is what we would play:

Family Game Night

What's better than family game night? Keeping track of the things that made it fun!

FAVORITE BOARD GAMES:

_____

_____

_____

_____

FAVORITE CARD GAMES:

_____

_____

_____

_____

THE USUAL WINNERS FOR EACH FAVORITE:

_____

_____

_____

_____

Screen Sharing

High-tech togetherness can be fun, too!
Here are gaming adventures we shared.

FAVORITE GAME APPS:

_____

_____

_____

FAVORITE CONSOLE GAMES:

_____

_____

_____

FAVORITE COMPUTER GAMES:

_____

_____

_____

a family secret
The best avatars and screen names we used:

Good Sports

Here are the types of sports our family
enjoyed watching or playing.

IN SPRING

Sports watched:_____

_____

Sports played & who played them:_____

_____

IN SUMMER

Sports watched:_____

_____

Sports played & who played them:_____

_____

IN FALL

Sports watched:_____

_____

Sports played & who played them:_____

_____

IN WINTER

Sports watched: _____

_____

Sports played & who played them: _____

_____

ANYTIME

This is a non-seasonal sport our family enjoyed: _____

_____

_____

_____

a family secret

An unofficial sport we invented just for our enjoyment:

Arts & Crafts

These kid creations hold a special place in our hearts.

Artist's name and age:

_____

About the artwork:

_____

_____

_____

Artist's name and age:

_____

About the artwork:

_____

_____

_____

Artist's name and age:

_____

About the artwork:

_____

_____

_____

_____

Artist's name and age:

_____

About the artwork:

_____

_____

_____

_____

_____

family fun

These are some favorite art teachers, classes, and events:

Club Connections

These are some favorite ways our family participated
in groups, and who was involved in each.

SCHOOL ORGANIZATIONS:

_____

_____

_____

_____

clubs for hobbies
and interests:

SCOUTING TROOPS:

_____

_____

_____

_____

_____

RELIGIOUS GROUPS:

COMMUNITY ORGANIZATIONS:

a family secret
This is a club we joked about starting:

Family means putting your arms around each other and being there.

—BARBARA BUSH

A

GLIMPSE

INTO

EVERYDAY

LIFE

At Our Best

Here is what we look like when we try our hardest.

BEST CAPTION FOR THIS PHOTO

_____, according to _____

_____, according to _____

_____, according to _____

_____, according to _____

_____, according to _____

_____, according to _____

No Filter

Here is how we look the *rest* of the time.

BEST CAPTION FOR THIS PHOTO

_____, according to _____

_____, according to _____

_____, according to _____

_____, according to _____

_____, according to _____

_____, according to _____

The Morning Routine

There's plenty to do before a family can head out the door. This is how it looks for us.

wake-up time for the parents:
_____ o'clock

wake-up time for the kids:
_____ o'clock

A LIST OF THINGS WE DO EACH MORNING:

_____

_____

_____

_____

THIS TRICK HAS HELPED US:

_____

_____

_____

_____

The Bedtime Routine

For us, good nights start something like this.

bedtime for the kids:
_____ o'clock

bedtime for the parents:
_____ o'clock

A LIST OF THINGS WE DO BEFORE BED:

_____

_____

_____

_____

THIS TRICK HAS HELPED US:

_____

_____

_____

_____

On the Menu

These are the foods that bring
everyone to the table at our home.

THE BREAKFAST CLUB

During the week: _____

On weekends: _____

For birthdays & special occasions: _____

_____

HOW WE DO LUNCH

During the week: _____

On weekends: _____

For birthdays & special occasions: _____

_____

OUR EVENING MEAL

During the week: _____

On weekends: _____

For birthdays & special occasions: _____

_____

SNACKS, SWEETS & SPECIAL TREATS

Favorite snack foods: _____

Favorite desserts: _____

Favorite candies: _____

Other treats: _____

a family secret
**The answer to "What's for dinner?"
that made the kids groan:**

Same or Different?

It's an unspoken rule: The children in one family must not all like the same things—or like the same things as their parents. Here are some ways we followed the rule.

FOOD & DRINK

Shared likes: _____

Shared dislikes: _____

Disagreed on: _____

ENTERTAINMENT (MUSIC, MOVIES & MORE)

Shared likes: _____

Shared dislikes: _____

Disagreed on: _____

SCHOOL & SUBJECTS

Shared likes: _____

Shared dislikes: _____

Disagreed on: _____

HOBBIES & INTERESTS

Shared likes: _____

Shared dislikes: _____

Disagreed on: _____

On the Go

We made memories in our second home on wheels.

THE CAR WE USED MOST:

Make: _____ Model: _____ Year: _____

ON A TYPICAL CAR RIDE, THE KIDS WOULD:

_____

WE PLAYED THESE GAMES IN THE CAR:

_____

ITEMS THAT WERE STOCKED IN THE CAR AT ALL TIMES:

_____

Best & Worst Parenting Moments

We may not always get it right, but we always try our best. Here's evidence of that—plus a few signature slipups.

OUR WALL OF FAME

Here are some moments that made us feel like good parents:

1.

2.

3.

What We Wish We'd Known

Here are some parenting lessons that we
learned the hard way. (Sorry, kids!)

A MEALTIME TIP:

A TRAVELING TIP:

A HOMEWORK TIP:

A BEHAVIOR TIP:

A COMMUNICATION TIP:

A TIP FOR THE TODDLER YEARS:

A TIP FOR GRADE SCHOOL:

A TIP FOR PARENTING TWEENS/TEENS:

Inside Jokes

We finish each other's sentences, laugh at things that don't seem funny, and generally "get" each other in ways only we understand.

FUNNY NAMES WE HAVE GIVEN
THINGS (OR EACH OTHER):

_____

_____

FAVORITE PHRASES WE QUOTE:

_____

_____

SOME THINGS WE TEASE EACH OTHER ABOUT:

_____

_____

A FUNNY FAMILY STORY WE TELL TIME AND AGAIN:

_____

_____

_____

_____

Notable Kid Quotables

Here are some of the best words of wisdom, mistakes, and observations that came out of kids in our family.

" _____ "

_____

— _____
WHO SAID IT

" _____ "

_____

— _____
WHO SAID IT

" _____ "

_____

— _____
WHO SAID IT

" _____ "

_____

— _____
WHO SAID IT

" _____ "

_____

— _____
WHO SAID IT

" _____ "

_____

— _____
WHO SAID IT

Things We Say & Do

Parents are quirky, too. These examples
are undeniable proof of it.

MOM ALWAYS SAYS:

_____

MOM ALWAYS DOES:

_____

MOM'S SILLIEST HABIT:

_____

DAD ALWAYS SAYS:

_____

DAD ALWAYS DOES:

_____

DAD'S SILLIEST HABIT:

_____

BETTER
TOGETHER

The Chore Chart

Cleaning, cooking, yard work, and more:
Here's how our little ones were a help
around the house in big and little ways.

Type of chore:

Starting age:

Type of chore:

Starting age:

Type of chore:

Starting age:

a family secret

These things were good motivators for the kids:

These things were not:

This is a chore that no one wanted to do:

84

Home Improvement

Every home needs a little TLC. Here are
some of the improvement projects we did—
and how the kids did (or didn't) help.

What needed fixing: _____

How we made it better: _____

How the kids helped: _____

What needed fixing: _____

How we made it better: _____

How the kids helped: _____

Our Helping Hands

Here are a few ways we shared our time,
talents, and treasures with those in need.

Who we helped: _____

How we helped: _____

Who we helped: _____

How we helped: _____

Who we helped: _____

How we helped: _____

WHAT OUR FAMILY CAN ACCOMPLISH FOR OTHERS WHEN WE WORK TOGETHER:

Ups & Downs

When the going gets tough, our family grows stronger. Here's how we have pulled through.

CHALLENGES & TRIUMPHS

One challenge we faced as a family:

_____

_____

how we responded:

What we learned from the experience:

_____

_____

BUMPS & BRUISES

Every family has its share of doctor visits. These are some of the more difficult health challenges we faced and how we supported each other.

_____

_____

Our Proudest Moments

At times, we realized we can do more than we thought.

ACTS OF HEROISM:

_____

_____

PERSONAL ACHIEVEMENTS:

_____

_____

HONORS AND AWARDS:

_____

_____

family fun
Everyday ways we cheer each other on:

Messages of Love

We love each other, but can we put it into words?

WHAT I LOVE ABOUT OUR FAMILY IS...

_____   _____
_____   _____
_____   _____

Says: _____   Says: _____

_____   _____
_____   _____
_____   _____

Says: _____   Says: _____

a family secret
The pet names or special gestures
we use to show our love :

Pictures That Say It All

Although it's impossible to capture the essence of our family in just moments, these photos express it best.

Date: _____ Special memory: _____

Date: _____ Special memory: _____

Date: _____ Special memory: _____

Date: _____ Special memory: _____

New Stages

Families naturally branch out and grow in new directions. Let's take a look into our family's future.

WHAT WE'RE LOOKING FORWARD TO WHEN THE KIDS ARE GROWN:

_____

_____

_____

_____

NEW THINGS WE'LL DO WITH OUR GROWN KIDS:

_____

_____

_____

_____

WHAT WE'RE LOOKING FORWARD TO AS OUR KIDS BEGIN FAMILIES OF THEIR OWN:

_____

_____

_____

_____